INGLÉS PARA NIÑOS

I SPEAK ENGLISH TOO! 2

Copyright © 2022 Zigzag English / Lydia Winter

All rights reserved. No part of this publication may be reproduced or transmitted in any form without the written permission of the author.

ISBN: 978-1-914911-17-0

www.zigzagenglish.co.uk

www.zigzagenglish.co.uk – BOOKS FOR ENGLISH LEARNERS
OUR BOOKS FOR CHILDREN

Our bilingual picture books for younger children. *Funny stories in simple, useful everyday English, with colour photos.*
English with Tony -1- Tony moves house
English with Tony -2- Tony is happy
English with Tony -3- Tony's Christmas
English with Tony -4- Tony's holiday
My best friend

Our coursebook for beginners *(age 7 to 11)*
English for Children - 1st Coursebook *(Essential vocabulary and grammar for beginners)*

Our dialogue books for beginners *(age 7 to 11).*
I Speak English Too! - 1
I Speak English Too! - 2

Our series of reading and comprehension books for beginners *(age 7 to 11).*
Read English with Zigzag - 1
Read English with Zigzag - 2
Read English with Zigzag - 3
   Audiobook at Audible.com

Our vocabulary book with photos, word puzzles and more *(age 7+)*
300+ mots en anglais / 300+ englische Wörter / 300+ palabras en inglés / 300+ parole inglesi

The Learn English Activity Book for Children *(A1 - A2, elementary).* *(Recommended for children in early secondary school.)*

Our series of reading and comprehension books for children at elementary level *(A1 - A2) (recommended for ages 10 to 13). With lots of language activities.*
Read English with Ben - 1
Read English with Ben - 2
Read English with Ben - 3

Our YOU DECIDE adventure book with 1 beginning and 19 endings. *A2 (11+)*   Your Bilingual Fairy Tale Adventure

Our series of reading and discussion books about a family with superpowers *(with writing tasks) for children at secondary school, A2 - B1*
I Live in a Castle – Book 1 – My Superpower
I Live in a Castle – Book 2 – The New Me

The Speak English, Read English, Write English Activity Books – *3 books from A1 to B2, for older children and adults.*

Our non-fiction book with language activities
Learn English with Fun Facts! – A2 - B2

English Dialogues for Teenagers – for ages 11 to 17, A2 - B2

OUR BOOKS FOR ADULTS

Our 3 Grammar books with grammar-focused dialogues
Learn English Grammar through Conversation – A1, A2 and B1

Our Dialogue books for adults *(with vocabulary lists and comprehension questions). Audiobooks are available for some of these books – at Audible.com.*
50 very Easy Everyday English Dialogues (A2)
50 Easy Everyday English Dialogues (A2 - B1)
50 Intermediate Everyday English Dialogues (B1 - B2)
50 more Intermediate Everyday English Dialogues (B1 - B2)
40 Advanced Everyday English Dialogues (B2 - C1)
40 Intermediate Business English Dialogues (B1 - B2)
40 Advanced Business English Dialogues (B2 - C1)

Our activity books for adults and older children
The Speak English, Read English, Write English Activity Books – 3 books, for A1 - A2, A2 - B1 and B1 - B2.

Our non-fiction book with language activities
Learn English with Fun Facts! – A2 - B2

Contents

Los objetivos de este libro son:	5
Nuestro método para enseñar inglés a niños de primaria:	5
Cómo usar este libro:	5
1A: Why's it boring?	7
2A: What are you good at?	12
3A: Mum says I can	16
4A: Who wants to be different?	21
5A: A swimming race	25
6A: I'm so tired	30
Word Search 1	35
7A: A history lesson	36
8A: A week's holiday	42
9A: It's spring	46
10A: A sleepover	51
11A: A concert	55
12A: I'm so happy	60
Word Search 2	62
Respuestas	63
Gracias por leer este libro.	65
From: Read English with Zigzag – 2	66
From: The Learn English Activity Book for children	67
From: Read English with Ben - 1	68

Los objetivos de este libro son:
1. Aumentar la confianza de tu hijo en la lectura y el habla de inglés.
2. Enseñarle palabras y frases clave y gramática para ayudarle a mejorar su uso del inglés.

Nuestro método para enseñar inglés a niños de primaria:
1. Estos diálogos fueron escritos por una profesora de inglés titulada y con experiencia y comprobado en niños de 7 a 12 años.
2. La forma más rápida de aprender un idioma es de manera individual. Si habla un poco de inglés, puede utilizar este libro para enseñarle a su hijo. No se preocupe por cometer errores - basta con leer las oraciones y las listas de vocabulario que aparecen en el libro. No obstante, puede llevar las cosas más allá utilizando los diálogos para crear y mantener nuevas conversaciones con su hijo.
3. Por supuesto, los diálogos también son aptos para hermanos y hermanas.
4. El libro parte del nivel pre-intermedio (que se alcanzó en el libro 1) y añade palabras y frases (con el siguiente nivel de gramática) para ampliar el inglés de su hijo. El niño tiene la oportunidad de aprender más con los diálogos "llenando los espacios" y con las preguntas de comprensión. También se pone a prueba el vocabulario en sopas de letras.
5. En 23 diálogos, su hijo pasará de "Maybe your school is fun. My school isn't." a saber decir "I can't believe you think singing is better than playing football."
6. Y entonces estará listo para pasar a conversaciones aún más complejas.

Cómo usar este libro:
1. Lea el <u>diálogo A</u> con su hijo.
2. Revisen la <u>lista de vocabulario</u> juntos.
3. Cambien roles y lean el diálogo nuevamente.
4. Anime a su hijo a realizar el ejercicio. La actividad "Fill the Gaps" puede hacerse sin ver las oraciones originales - este es un reto divertido, que permitirá al niño utilizar cualquier palabra que tenga sentido dentro del diálogo. O lo que es más fácil, puede pedirle a su hijo que vea las oraciones que faltan - están al final del ejercicio - y que escoja las correctas.

5. Las respuestas a las preguntas de comprensión de los diálogos 2, 4, 6, 8 y 10 se encuentran al final del libro.
6. Lean el diálogo B. Cambien roles. Hágale a su hijo las preguntas de C: "What about you?"
7. Si usted habla inglés, intente conversar con su hijo utilizando el lenguaje en los diálogos A y B, así como el lenguaje de diálogos anteriores. Por supuesto también puede incluir algunas palabras y frases nuevas si así lo desea. Desde nuestro punto de vista, esta es la manera más efectiva de enseñarle inglés a un niño. Ayudará a su hijo a mejorar su uso del inglés día a día.
8. A medida que el inglés de su hijo mejore, intente incluir algunos libros y audiolibros sencillos y animar a su hijo a ver televisión para niños. ¿Por qué no prueba nuestra serie de 3 libros de lectura progresiva en inglés para principiantes: ***Read English with Zigzag?*** Trata sobre un gato, un perro, un hermano y una hermana. ¡Es divertido y tiene muchos dibujos! También incluye listas de vocabulario, preguntas de comprensión y divertidas actividades lingüísticas. También hay un **audiolibro**.
9. Ver un niño pasar de hablar un inglés muy básico a comunicarse a un nivel más útil es algo maravilloso. ¡Buena suerte y diviértanse!

LESSON 1

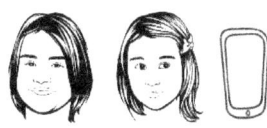

1A: Why's it boring?

Anna: Are you **back** at school now, Katie?

Katie: Yes, I am. It's so boring!

Anna: Why's it boring?

Katie: I go to school every **morning**. I have **the same** teacher every day. I see the same friends. In the afternoon, I go home and do my homework. Of course it's boring.

Anna: School's not boring. It's quite **fun**.

Katie: Maybe your school is fun. My school isn't.

Anna: But you don't really go to school every day. You don't go to school on Saturday or Sunday, do you?

Katie: No, I don't go to school at the weekend. But I go to school on Monday, Tuesday, Wednesday, Thursday and Friday!

Anna: I like school. I like seeing my friends and **learning** new things.

Katie: You're right. School's not too bad. But **holidays** are better.

Anna: When's your next holiday?

Katie: In six **weeks**. **I can't wait**!

Vocabulary
- back — de vuelta
- morning — mañana
- the same — lo mismo
- fun — divertido
- to learn — aprender
- holiday — vacaciones
- week — semana
- I can't wait — No veo la hora

1A: Fill the gaps

Anna: Are you back at school now, Katie?

Katie:

Anna: Why's it boring?

Katie:

Anna: School's not boring. It's quite fun.

Katie:

Anna: But you don't really go to school every day. You don't go to school on Saturday or Sunday, do you?

Katie: No, I don't go to school at the weekend. But I go to school on Monday, Tuesday, Wednesday, Thursday and Friday!

Anna:

Katie: You're right. School's not too bad. But holidays are better.

Anna:

Katie: In six weeks. I can't wait!

1. Maybe your school is fun. My school isn't.
2. When's your next holiday?
3. I like school. I like seeing my friends and learning new things.
4. I go to school every morning. I have the same teacher every day. I see the same friends. In the afternoon, I go home and do my homework. Of course it's boring.
5. Yes, I am. It's so boring!

1B: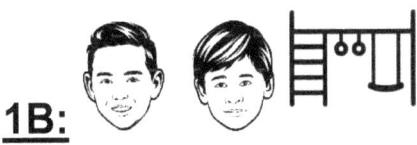

Sam: What do you do **after** school, Jack? Do you **just** go home?

Jack: Sometimes I go home. But sometimes I do **sport**.

Sam: What sport do you do?

Jack: I **play** football.

Sam: When?

Jack: I play football on Monday.

Sam: I play football too. But not on Monday, on Wednesday. Do you play football at school?

Jack: No, I play at a football club. Where do you play?

Sam: I play at school. And I often play at the park too, with friends.

Jack: I do judo too. I love judo.

Sam: I don't do judo, but I do karate. Karate's fun. I do karate on Thursday.

Jack: What do you do on Friday?

Sam: I'm **usually tired**, so I **watch television** with my family.

Vocabulary
- after — después de
- just — sólo
- sport — deporte
- to play — jugar
- usually — normalmente
- tired — cansado
- to watch television — ver la televisión

1C: What about you?

1. *What's better – school or holidays?*
2. *What do you do after school?*
3. *What's your favourite sport?*

LESSON 2

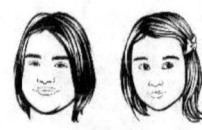

2A: What are you good at?

Anna: If you think school is boring, why don't you do **something** after school?

Katie: Like what?

Anna: Like sport, maybe?

Katie: I'm bad at sport. Are you **good at** it?

Anna: I'm **pretty** good at **swimming**. I'm in a swimming club.

Katie: How often do you go swimming? Every week?

Anna: I go swimming **twice** a week – on Tuesdays and Thursdays.

Katie: That's **too much** swimming. And I'm not very good at it.

Anna: So what ARE you good at?

Katie: I don't know. I quite like **singing**.

Anna: Why don't you **join** a **choir** then?

Katie: That's a good idea. Thanks, Anna!

Vocabulary
- something   algo
- good at   bueno en
- pretty   bastante
- swimming   natación
- twice   dos veces
- too much   demasiado
- singing   cantar
- to join   unirse a
- choir   coro

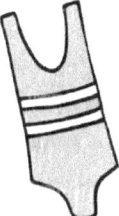

-

2A: Find the right answer

1. What is Katie good at?
    a. She's good at swimming.
    b. She's good at singing.
    c. She doesn't know what she's good at.

2. How often does Anna go swimming?
    a. She goes swimming three times a week.
    b. Twice a week.
    c. Once a week

3. What is Katie bad at?
   a. She's bad at English.
   b. Singing.
   c. She's bad at sport.

2B:

Sam: **What's wrong**, Jack?

Jack: **Nothing**. Why?

Sam: I don't know. You don't look very **happy**.

Jack: I'm fine.

Sam: Really?

Jack: Okay, I'm not fine. My mum wants me to…

Sam: What?

Jack: My mum thinks I do too much sport.

Sam: Too much sport?!

Jack: Yes. She wants me **to stop** playing football.

Sam: That's bad.

Jack: Yes, I know. And that's not all. She wants me to…

Sam: What?

Jack: She wants me to **try** singing. She wants me to join a choir.

Sam: Oh no!

Vocabulary
- wrong   mal
- nothing   nada
- happy   feliz
- to stop   dejar de
- to try   probar

2C: What about you?

1. *What are you good at?*
2. *What are you bad at?*
3. *Do you do too much sport?*

LESSON 3

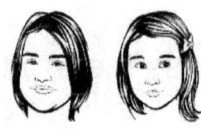

3A: Mum says I can

Anna: So how's school, Katie? Is it **still** boring?

Katie: Yes, it's still a bit boring.

Anna: What about after school?

Katie: That's a bit **more interesting**. My mum says I can join a choir!

Anna: Really? That's great!

Katie: Yes, it is, isn't it?

Anna: Is there a choir at your school?

Katie: No, there's not. There isn't a choir at my school, but there's a children's choir in Cambridge. It's for children from 8 to 13.

Anna: That's **perfect**.

Katie: Yes, it's **just right** for me.

Anna: When do you start?

Katie: **Next week**. I can't wait!

Anna: Let's **talk again** next week. I want to know **how it goes**.

Vocabulary
- still — todavía
- more — más
- interesting — interesante
- perfect — perfecto
- just right — justo
- next week — la próxima semana
- to talk — hablar
- again — de nuevo
- how it goes — cómo va

3A: Fill the gaps

Anna:

Katie: Yes, it's still a bit boring.

Anna:

Katie: That's a bit more interesting. My mum says I can join a choir!

Anna: Really? That's great!

Katie:

Anna:

Katie: No, there's not. There isn't a choir at my school, but there's a children's choir in Cambridge. It's for children from 8 to 13.

Anna:

Katie: Yes, it's just right for me.

Anna: When do you start?

Katie:

Anna: Let's talk again next week. I want to know how it goes.

1. Next week. I can't wait!
2. Is there a choir at your school?
3. That's perfect.
4. What about after school?
5. Yes, it is, isn't it?
6. So how's school, Katie? Is it still boring?

3B:

Jack: So how's football?

Sam: It's good, thanks. Are you still playing football?

Jack: No, I'm not. I can't play football **anymore**.

Sam: **I'm** really **sorry**.

Jack: I'm sorry too. I'm so **angry** with my mum. She knows I love football.

Sam: What does your dad **say**?

Jack: He thinks mum's right. He wants me to do **less** sport. He wants me to try singing.

Sam: Are you good at singing?

Jack: I don't know. Mum and dad think I am. That's why they want me to join a choir.

Sam: Is there a choir at your school?

Jack: There is a choir at school, but it's really bad. So my parents want me to join a choir in **town**.

Sam: What choir? What's its name?

Jack: It's called The City of Cambridge Children's Choir.

Sam: When do you start?

Jack: **Tomorrow**!

Vocabulary
- anymore — más
- I'm sorry — lo siento
- angry — enojado
- to say — decir

- less   menos
- town   ciudad
- tomorrow   mañana

3C: What about you?

1. *Do you sing in a choir?*
2. *How often do you play football?*
3. *Is there a choir at your school?*

LESSON 4

4A: Who wants to be different?

Katie: Is this where the children's choir is?

Jack: I don't know. **Probably**.

Katie: Are you new too?

Jack: Yes. I don't really want to be here.

Katie: Why not? I'm **excited**!

Jack: Singing's okay for girls, but **I'd rather** be at football.

Katie: My mum says there are lots of boys in the choir. And it's a **chance** to make some new friends.

Jack: I **already** have friends, thanks.

Katie: Why are you here, then?

Jack: Because of my mum. My dad, too. They want me to learn to sing.

Katie: They're right. Every boy I know plays football. Why not do something a bit different?

Jack: I like doing the same things as my friends. Who wants to be different?

Katie: I think trying different things is interesting. It's nearly seven o'clock. Where are all the **other** children?

Jack: Look – **over there**. That's where they are. Let's go.

Vocabulary
- different   diferente
- probably   probablemente
- excited   emocionado
- I'd rather   prefiero
- chance   oportunidad
- already   ya
- other   otro
- over there   allí

4A: Find the right answer

1. Why doesn't Jack want to be at choir?
    a. Because he doesn't like girls.
    b. Because he'd rather be at football.
    c. Because he doesn't want to learn to sing.

2. How many boys are there in the choir?
    a. There are no boys in the choir.
    b. There are lots of boys in the choir.
    c. There are three or four boys in the choir.

3. Do Jack and Katie want to do something different?
    a. Jack does, but Katie doesn't. Jack likes trying new things.
    b. No. Katie wants to do the same things as her friends.
    c. Katie does, but Jack doesn't. Katie thinks it's interesting to try new things.

4B

Anna: Do you like the choir?

Katie: Yes, I think so. The singing is quite **hard**, **though**.

Anna: Are the other children all good singers?

Katie: They're not bad. It's a good choir.

Anna: How big is it?

Katie: It's very big. There are **almost** sixty children.

Anna: How many girls and how many boys?

Katie: There are **about** forty girls and twenty boys. That's because **so many** boys just want to play football.

Anna: It's the same here. Are the other children in the choir nice?

Katie: I don't know **yet**. There is one boy I like, though.

Anna: Really? Who's that?

Katie: He's called Jack. He's new, too, but he's a good singer. He's much **better than** me.

Vocabulary
- hard   duro
- though   aunque
- almost   casi
- about   unas
- so many   tantos
- yet   todavía
- better than   mejor que

4C: What about you?

1. Do you think trying something new is boring or interesting?
2. Do you like the same things as your friends, or do you like different things?
3. Do the boys at your school like singing? Why? / Why not?

LESSON 5

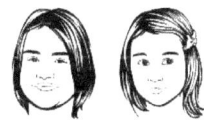

5A: A swimming race

Katie: So how are things in Madrid?

Anna: Not bad. But I'm really **busy**.

Katie: Why?

Anna: I have a lot of work at school. The teachers give us lots of homework **now**.

Katie: **What about** your swimming? Are you still doing that?

Anna: Yes. I don't want to stop swimming. I like it a lot.

Katie: Are you in a **team**?

Anna: Yes. And we have a **competition** soon.

Katie: How many races are you in?

Anna: Just one **race**. I'm in the girls' **backstroke** race.

Katie: How far do you **have to** swim?

Anna: I have to swim 50 metres. And I have to swim very **fast**. It's **exhausting**.

Katie: When's the race?

Anna: It's in two weeks!

Katie: That's so **soon**. Are you excited?

Anna: I'm a bit **scared**. I don't want to come **last**!

Vocabulary
- busy — ocupado
- now — ahora
- what about — qué hay de
- team — equipo
- competition — competición
- race — carrera
- backstroke — espalda
- to have to — tener que
- fast — rápido
- exhausting — agotadora
- soon — pronto
- I'm scared — tengo miedo
- last — último

5A: Fill the gaps

Katie: So how are things in Madrid?

Anna: Not bad. But I'm really busy.
Katie: Why?

Anna:

Katie: What about your swimming? Are you still doing that?

Anna:

Katie: Are you in a team?

Anna: Yes. And we have a competition soon.

Katie:

Anna: Just one race. I'm in the girls' backstroke race.

Katie: How far do you have to swim?

Anna:

Katie:

Anna: It's in two weeks!

Katie: That's so soon. Are you excited?

Anna:

1. Yes. I don't want to stop swimming. I like it a lot.
2. How many races are you in?
3. When's the race?
4. I'm a bit scared. I don't want to come last!
5. I have a lot of work at school. The teachers give us lots of homework now.

6. I have to swim 50 metres. And I have to swim very fast. It's exhausting.

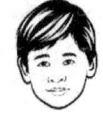
5B:

Sam: It's quite warm today. Do you think it's **spring** now?

Jack: I **hope** so. I hate cold **weather**.

Sam: What are you doing this weekend?

Jack: Nothing. Just homework. Why?

Sam: Do you want to play football?

Jack: Football? You know I don't play football now.

Sam: I know you don't play football at your football club. But can't you play with me and my friends? We play in the park. It's fun.

Jack: I don't know. What about my parents?

Sam: You don't have to **tell** them, do you?

Jack: Yes, okay. I really want to play some football. I **miss** it.

Sam: Good. **See you** on Saturday afternoon at the park.

Jack: Yes. See you!

Vocabulary
- spring — primavera
- to hope — esperar
- weather — el tiempo
- to tell — decir a
- to miss — echar de menos
- see you — nos vemos

5C: What about you?

1. Are you in a team? What team are you in?
2. Do your teachers give you lots of homework?
3. Do you hate cold weather or hot weather?

LESSON 6

6A: I'm so tired

Katie: Are you having a good week, Anna?

Anna: Not bad. I'm busy. I'm swimming every day at the moment.

Katie: Every day? Don't you go swimming twice a week?

Anna: I usually go swimming twice a week, but it's the swimming competition next week, so I have to do more **training**.

Katie: When do you go swimming? In the morning or in the afternoon? **Before** school or after school?

Anna: I usually go swimming after school. But sometimes I go swimming at **lunchtime**.

Katie: Do you have **time** to go swimming *and* have lunch?

Anna: No, not really. When I go swimming at lunchtime, my mum **makes** me a sandwich. Sometimes I buy some chocolate, too.

Katie: You're **working so hard!**

Anna: Yes, it's really **tiring**. I have to go to bed early because I'm so tired. But I can **relax** after the competition.

Katie: When is the competition? Is it at the weekend?

Anna: No, it's next Thursday **evening**.

Katie: I have to go now – mum says it's dinner time. Good luck in the competition, Anna!

Anna: Thanks!

Vocabulary
- training — entrenamiento
- before — antes de
- lunchtime — la hora del almuerzo
- time — tiempo
- to make — hacer
- to work hard — trabajar duro
- tiring — agotador
- to relax — relajarse
- evening — noche

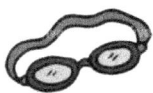 

6A: Answer the questions

1. How often does Anna usually go swimming, and how often is she going swimming at the moment?
2. Does she go swimming before school?
3. What does Anna want to do after the swimming competition?

6B:

Jack: Hi, Sam. Where are your friends?

Sam: Thanks for coming, Jack. My friends are over there, **under** the **tree**.

Jack: Are they all boys?

Sam: No, there are two or three girls. Lots of my friends are girls, but they don't all play football.

Jack: Are they waiting for us?

Sam: I think so. It's half past three – time to play football.

Jack: Is your best friend here?

Sam: Yes. Daniel's the boy who's **kicking** the ball. He wants to start playing!

Jack: Is it **his** ball?

Sam: Yes, he always **brings** the ball.

Jack: Are your friends all good at football?

Sam: Some of them are very good at football. But some of them don't play very often, so they're not very good at it. **It doesn't matter**. We're just playing for fun.

Jack: You're right. Not **everything** has to be a competition.

Vocabulary
- under — bajo
- tree — árbol
- to kick — patear
- his — su
- to bring — traer
- it doesn't matter — no importa
- everything — todo

6C: What about you?

1. Do you play football? Where do you play it?
2. Do you have a football? Where is it?
3. How many of your friends are boys, and how many are girls?

Word Search 1

```
Q J S N H Z J H Y Q A X O T M
V S Q I U O R F U E E C M O B
W H P V S I H O L I D A Y M T
I X P T U V D A T R O R L O H
I Q S C A R E D C X T F H R W
V W F O L L U Y N Z J V S R E
G P G Y L W U F N X N F M O T
U E K U Y E X C I T E D K W V
P A W M A A J P R O B A B L Y
T I R E D T B E T T E R H F K
W I B G S H F R V S D B A B V
I Y Z A T E Z F H R S V R Q P
C O S P O R G E R H T O D W T
E K W M Q V Z C R A R D J Y L
W P H X F J R T J T T N N C Q
```

- I'm so **ex_i_ed**! I'm going on **h_l_d_y to_o_r_w**!
- What's the **we_th_r** like in the summer? It's **us_al_y** too hot.
- What's **b_tt_r** than coming second? Coming first!
- You look really **t_red**. You're **pro_a_ly** working too **_ar_**.
- It's the swimming competition tomorrow. I'm **sc_r_d**!
- I love my new school. It's **p_rf_ct**!
- I'm in a football club. I play football **tw_c_** a week.

LESSON 7

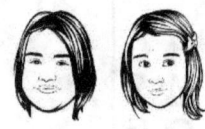

7A: A history lesson

Katie: So how did the competition go, Anna? Did you win?

Anna: No, I didn't. I didn't **win**, and I didn't come second, **either**. But I came third. I'm happy with that. Coming third is much, much better than coming last.

Katie: That's a great **result. Well done**!

Anna: Thanks. I can relax now. It's nice not to have to go swimming every day. What about you? How is school going?

Katie: It's going okay. I'm **enjoying history lessons at the moment**. History isn't usually very interesting, but we're learning some really interesting things at the moment.

Anna: Like what?

Katie: We're learning **about** Guy Fawkes.

Anna: What's that?

Katie: It's a man's name. He's **famous** in the UK.

Anna: Why is he famous?

Katie: He's famous for trying **to kill** the king. It's because of him that we all **celebrate** on the fifth of November.

Anna: What **kind** of celebration is it?

Katie: We usually have a big **bonfire**, with **fireworks**.

Anna: That sounds fun. I love fireworks.

Katie: Me too. My mum thinks they're **dangerous**, but my dad always buys some for Bonfire **Night**.

Anna: Bonfire Night?

Katie: The fifth of November, **remember**?

Vocabulary
- to win   ganar
- either   tampoco
- result   resultado
- well done   bien hecho
- to enjoy   disfrutar
- history   historia
- lesson   lección
- at the moment   por el momento
- about   sobre
- famous   famoso
- to kill   matar
- to celebrate   celebrar

- kind — tipo
- bonfire — hoguera
- firework — fuego artificial
- dangerous — peligroso
- night — noche
- remember — recordar

7A: Fill the gaps

Katie:

Anna: No, I didn't. I didn't win, and I didn't come second, either. But I came third. I'm happy with that. Coming third is much, much better than coming last.

Katie:

Anna: Thanks. I can relax now. It's nice not to have to go swimming every day. What about you? How is school going?

Katie: It's going okay. I'm enjoying history lessons at the moment. History isn't usually very interesting, but we're learning some really interesting things at the moment.

Anna:

Katie: We're learning about Guy Fawkes.

Anna: What's that?

Katie:

Anna: Why is he famous?

Katie: He's famous for trying to kill the king. It's because of him that we all celebrate on the fifth of November.

Anna: What kind of celebration is it?

Katie:

Anna:

Katie: Me too. My mum thinks they're dangerous, but my dad always buys some for Bonfire Night.

Anna: Bonfire Night?

Katie:

1. That's a great result. Well done!
2. It's a man's name. He's famous in the UK.
3. The fifth of November, remember?
4. Like what?
5. So how did the competition go, Anna? Did you win?
6. That sounds fun. I love fireworks.
7. We usually have a big bonfire, with fireworks.

7B:

Sam: What are you doing this weekend, Jack?

Jack: I don't know. Probably not much. My mum and dad are working this weekend, so I can do what I want.

Sam: So can you just sit on the sofa, watch television and play **computer games** all weekend?

Jack: I **need** to do some homework. And I'm reading some manga.

Sam: I like manga, too. Can you **draw** manga?

Jack: No, I don't know how to. Why, can you?

Sam: A bit. It's not too hard. Lots of my friends draw manga. I usually draw manga at the weekend.

Jack: I'm not very good at **art**, but I like **writing.** I'm writing a **song**.

Sam: A song? **What do you mean**?

Jack: I'm writing a new song for my choir.

Vocabulary
- computer game   juego de ordenador
- to need   necesitar
- to draw   dibujar
- art   arte
- to write   escribir
- song   canción
- What do you mean?   ¿Qué quieres decir?

7C: What about you?

1. What's your favourite celebration?
2. Do you sometimes play computer games all weekend?
3. Do you think drawing manga is hard?

LESSON 8

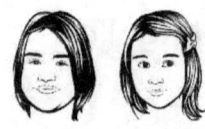

8A: A week's holiday

Katie: It's my **half term holiday** next week. A **whole** week with no school!

Anna: Are you **going away**?

Katie: Yes. We're going to the Lake District.

Anna: What's that? Where is it?

Katie: It's in the **north** of England. There are lots of **mountains** and **lakes**. It's very beautiful.

Anna: Lucky you! I have school next week.

Katie: School is really hard at the moment. I'm tired. I need a **break**.

Anna: Is your whole family going?

Katie: No. My mum has to work next week. So she's **staying** at home.

Anna: Your **poor** mum.

Katie: **She doesn't mind** too much. She says she wants to have a nice **quiet** week with lots of television. And she wants **to go out** with some friends.

Anna: Does your mum have lots of friends?

Katie: Yes, she's really popular. But she's usually too busy to go out with them very often. She says that next week is a chance to have some "me time".

Anna: What does "me time" mean?

Katie: It means she **only** has to think about **herself**. No children or **husband** to **worry** about!

Vocabulary
- half term   mitad de trimestre
- whole   completo
- we're going away nos vamos a ir
- north   norte
- mountain   montaña
- lake   lago
- break   descanso
- to stay   quedarse
- poor   pobre
- she doesn't mind no le importa
- quiet   tranquilo
- to go out   salir
- only   sólo
- herself   ella misma
- husband   marido
- to worry   preocuparse

8A: Answer the questions

1. Where's the Lake District?
2. Why isn't Katie's mum going on holiday?
3. Why doesn't Katie's mum have time to see her friends very often?

8B:

Sam: So how's your half term going?

Jack: We're not going away this time, so it's a bit boring.

Sam: We're not going away either. Well, we are, but only for three days.

Jack: Where are you going?

Sam: **Nowhere** exciting. Just to my grandparents' house.

Jack: Where do they live? **Somewhere** nice?

Sam: They live in London. It's not far. I like going to London. There's so much to see and do there.

Jack: Yes, London's really exciting. But my dad says it's too expensive. So we don't go there very often.

Sam: I'm lucky my grandparents live there. So it's cheap for us. They usually **pay** for everything.

Jack: What's your favourite thing to do in London?

Sam: I don't know. Probably the London **Dungeon**.

Jack: Why is it your favourite?

Sam: Because it's **dark** and very **scary**. It's fun!

Vocabulary
- nowhere — ningún lugar
- somewhere — algún lugar
- to pay — pagar
- dungeon — mazmorra
- dark — oscuro
- scary — de terror

8C: What about you?

1. Where do you like going on holiday?
2. How busy is your mum?
3. How often do you go to Madrid? Or do you live in Madrid?

LESSON 9

9A: It's spring

Anna: Did you have a nice holiday?

Katie: Yes and no.

Anna: What do you mean?

Katie: The Lake District is lovely. But there's not very much to do there, if you don't like walking.

Anna: Don't you like walking?

Katie: Not walking up enormous mountains, no! There are lakes, too, but you can't swim in them in February – the **water**'s too cold.

Anna: So are you happy to be back at school?

Katie: Happy to be at school? That's very **funny**. We're getting so much homework.

Anna: **At least** it's spring now. What's spring like in Cambridge?

Katie: It's lovely here now. It's not too cold, and there are **flowers everywhere**.

Anna: What do you like **best**, spring or **summer**?

Katie: Spring, I think. It's not too hot, and there aren't too many tourists.

Anna: I know what you mean. We get **loads** of **tourists** in Madrid too!

Vocabulary
- water — agua
- funny — gracioso
- at least — al menos
- flower — flor
- everywhere — en todas partes
- best — mejor
- summer — verano
- tourist — turista
- loads — un montón de

9A: Fill the gaps

Anna:

Katie: Yes and no.

Anna:

Katie: The Lake District is lovely. But there's not very much to do there, if you don't like walking.

Anna:

Katie: Not walking up enormous mountains, no! There are lakes, too, but you can't swim in them in February – the water's too cold.

Anna: So are you happy to be back at school?

Katie:

Anna: At least it's spring now. What's spring like in Cambridge?

Katie:

Anna:

Katie: Spring, I think. It's not too hot, and there aren't too many tourists.

Anna:

1. It's lovely here now. It's not too cold, and there are flowers everywhere.
2. What do you mean?
3. Don't you like walking?
4. Happy to be at school? That's very funny. We're getting so much homework.
5. Did you have a nice holiday?
6. I know what you mean. We get loads of tourists in Madrid too!
7. What do you like best, spring or summer?

9B:

Sam: Do you know what day it is tomorrow?

Jack: Umm…, Tuesday?

Sam: It's **Pancake** Day! My school is having a pancake race.

Jack: You mean when you have to run and **toss** a pancake with your **frying pan** at the same time?

Sam: Yes. It's good fun.

Jack: Are you any good at tossing pancakes?

Sam: They don't **use real** pancakes. They use tortillas. Tossing a tortilla is **easier than** tossing a pancake.

Jack: That's **cheating**!

Sam: **I suppose so**. But after school I make pancakes with my mum, so I toss those.

Jack: What do you put on your pancakes? **Lemon juice** and **sugar**?

Sam: Or chocolate **sauce** with bananas and ice cream.

Jack: That sounds **amazing**!

Vocabulary
- pancake — panqueque
- to toss — tirar
- frying pan — sartén
- to use — usar
- real — de verdad
- easier than — más fácil que
- to cheat — hacer trampas
- I suppose so — supongo que sí
- lemon juice — zumo de limón
- sugar — azúcar
- sauce — salsa
- amazing — increíble

9C: What about you?

1. What day is it tomorrow?
2. What do you put on YOUR pancakes?
3. Do you like spring or summer best? Why?

LESSON 10

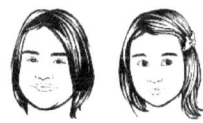

10A: A sleepover

Anna: I'm sorry you don't live in Madrid, Katie.

Katie: I'm sorry, too. Madrid is much more exciting than Cambridge. But why are you sorry I don't live in Madrid?

Anna: Because you're so far away. I'm having a **sleepover** tomorrow, but of course you can't come.

Katie: That's really **unfair**. I never see you, and I love sleepovers.

Anna: Me too. Sara's coming, and two other friends. We're watching a scary **film** and my mum's making an enormous pizza.

Katie: That sounds great. You know, Anna, you can come and stay with me in Cambridge whenever you want.

Anna: What do you mean? For a holiday?

Katie: Yes. Why not?

Anna: What does your mum say?

Katie: My parents love having **visitors**. **Especially people** from other **countries**. They say it's interesting.

Anna: And my parents always want me to speak English.

Katie: When you come and stay with me, you can speak English all day, every day!

Vocabulary
- sleepover   pijamada
- unfair   injusto
- film   película
- visitor   visitante
- especially   especialmente
- people   gente
- country   país

10A: Answer the questions

1. Why do Katie's parents love having visitors from other countries?
2. Why can't Katie go to Anna's sleepover?
3. What does Katie want Anna to do?

10B:

Jack: I have a **maths test** tomorrow.

Sam: So?

Jack: It's a really important one.

Sam: Aren't you good at maths?

Jack: No, not really. I'm a bit worried.

Sam: Tests are scary. But if you do badly, it doesn't really matter.

Jack: What do you mean, it doesn't matter?

Sam: I mean, the school can't **punish** you.

Jack: The school can't punish me, but my parents can!

Sam: Do your parents punish you if you do badly at school?

Jack: Not usually. But maths tests are important.

Sam: Why are they so important?

Jack: Because my parents want me to go to **private school** when I **finish primary school**. But I can only go if I'm really good at maths and English.

Sam: I'm just going to the **secondary school** near my house. **Anyone** who lives near the school can go there. And my parents don't have to pay!

Vocabulary
- maths — matemáticas
- test — examen
- to punish — castigar
- private school — escuela privada
- to finish — terminar
- primary school — escuela primaria
- secondary school — escuela secundaria
- anyone — cualquiera

10C: What about you?

1. *Do you think sleepovers are popular in your country?*
2. *How good are you at maths?*
3. *Do you enjoy tests, or do you think they're scary?*

LESSON 11

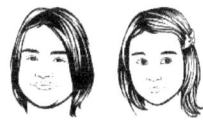

11A: A concert

Katie: I want to tell you something.

Anna: What?

Katie: I'm in a **concert** next week.

Anna: What kind of concert?

Katie: A choir concert. It's my first choir concert.

Anna: Are you excited?

Katie: I think I am. It's pretty exciting. We all have to wear the same clothes – black skirts or trousers and blue tops.

Anna: And what are you singing?

Katie: All kinds of songs. Pop songs, jazz songs and **classical** songs.

Anna: Is the boy you like still in the choir? Is he singing in the concert too?

Katie: Jack? Yes, of course he is. He's a fantastic singer now. He's singing a solo.

Anna: Is **everyone** in your family going to the concert?

Katie: My sister doesn't want to go, but mum says she has to.

Anna: Well, good luck in the concert!

Katie: Thanks!

Vocabulary
- concert   concierto
- classical   clásico
- everyone   todos

11A: Fill the gaps

Katie: I want to tell you something.

Anna:

Katie: I'm in a concert next week.

Anna:

Katie: A choir concert. It's my first choir concert.

Anna: Are you excited?

Katie: I think I am. It's pretty exciting. We all have to wear the same clothes – black skirts or trousers and blue tops.

Anna:

Katie: All kinds of songs. Pop songs, jazz songs and classical songs.

Anna: Is the boy you like still in the choir? Is he singing in the concert too?

Katie:

Anna: Is everyone in your family going to the concert?

Katie:

Anna:

Katie: Thanks!

1. And what are you singing?
2. Well, good luck in the concert!
3. Jack? Yes, of course he is. He's a fantastic singer now. He's singing a solo.
4. What kind of concert?
5. My sister doesn't want to go, but mum says she has to.
6. What?

11B:

Jack: Now the maths test is over, I can think about something nicer.

Sam: **Like what**?

Jack: Like the concert tomorrow.

Sam: What? You're in a concert?

Jack: Yes. I'm singing in a concert with my choir.

Sam: So you're still in the choir, then?

Jack: Yes, why not? I love the choir. It's better than judo. It's even better than football!

Sam: I can't believe you think singing is better than playing football.

Jack: Singing with fifty other people is lots of fun; and I love the music.

Sam: The good thing is, if you're singing with fifty other people, no-one can **hear** you if you make a **mistake**.

Jack: They can if you sing a solo.

Sam: But solos are for the really good singers.

Jack: Well, I'm singing a solo tomorrow night.

Vocabulary
- like what? ¿Cómo qué?
- to hear escuchar
- mistake error

11C: What about you?

1. How often do you go to concerts?
2. What kind of music do you like?
3. Do you think singing a solo is scary or fun?

LESSON 12

12A: I'm so happy

Jack: Where is everyone? Is this the right **place**?

Katie: I think so. What time is it?

Jack: It's a quarter to seven. Are we too early?

Katie: The concert starts at eight o'clock. So yes, we probably are too early.

Jack: How many people are coming to hear you sing?

Katie: My family. That's three people.

Jack: Lots of people are coming to hear me. My parents, my grandparents, my **uncle** and **aunt** and two **cousins**. I think **a few** of my friends are coming too.

Katie: That's because you're singing a solo.

Jack: Yes, I know. I'm **feeling** really **nervous**.

Katie: You don't need to worry. You're so good at singing.

Jack: Thanks. I'm so happy I'm in the choir.

Katie: So am I. And maybe if I work hard I can sing a solo **next time**.

Vocabulary
- place   lugar
- uncle   tío
- aunt   tía
- cousin   primo
- a few   unos pocos
- to feel   sentirse
- nervous   nervioso
- next time   la próxima vez

12B: What about you?

1. *Do you want to join a choir?*
2. *How many cousins do you have? Are they girls or boys?*
3. *When do you feel nervous?*

Word Search 2

```
G M U O B C Q U I E T C N V F
Q P U C H M B W U V W O E N U
V T N W E Z W E I T G U Z V N
F C C R I I P D M V F N A Z N
U K D A E X P V K T G T R W Y
C Q R I W O D C M G Y R T D N
O O K J X F A M O U S Y I W F
C H E A P I N F M A H O I K Z
V I V M O R G Z M F Z L E Y Q
X N O A P E E L K X R I B L W
A V Y Z U W R V R X E Q B I A
F S M I L O O K Q S C A R Y T
X D B N A R U I O Y F Z R Y C
R Q B G R K S Q J X Z J O U H
E X P E N S I V E N X E U I V
```

- On Bonfire Night, we always **w_tch** the **f_r_w_rks**. They're **am_z_ng**. But it's a bit **_c_ry**, because my dad says they're **d_ng_r_us**.
- I want to buy this jacket. But is it **_hea_** or **_xp_ns_v_**?
- My best friend is a very **qu_et** girl. But she's quite **p_p_l_r**. She has lots of friends.
- Guy Fawkes is **f_mou_** in the UK because he tried to kill the king. Who is **f_mou_** in your **co_n_ry**?
- I like my teacher. He's so 😆 !

Respuestas

Dialogue 2A: Find the right answer

1: c
2: b
3: c

Dialogue 4A: Find the right answer

1: b
2: b
3: c

Dialogue 6A: Answer the questions

1: She usually goes swimming twice a week, but at the moment she's going swimming every day.
2: No, she doesn't. She goes swimming after school and at lunchtime.
3: She wants to relax.

Dialogue 8A Answer the questions

1: It's in the north of England.
2: Because she has to work.
3: Because she's usually too busy.

Dialogue 10A: Answer the questions

1: Because they think it's interesting.
2: Because Katie lives too far away. She lives in England and Anna lives in Spain.
3: Katie wants Anna to stay with her, for a holiday.

Gracias por leer este libro.

Si tiene alguna pregunta sobre este libro, envíenosla y nos pondremos en contacto con usted lo antes posible. Si tiene alguna sugerencia para la próxima edición de este libro, o para otros libros que le gustaría que publicáramos para ayudar a su hijo a aprender inglés, nos encantaría escucharla.
Escríbanos a: lydiawinter.zigzagenglish@gmail.com

Puede echar un vistazo a nuestros otros libros para niños y adultos, jugar a algunos juegos en inglés y leer nuestro blog, en:
www.zigzagenglish.co.uk.

Por favor...
Escribe una reseña sobre este libro. Las reseñas son importantes para otros padres y también para nosotros. Gracias.

Aquí tiene algunos extractos de nuestros otros libros para niños que empiezan a aprender inglés:

From: Read English with Zigzag – 2

11 I'm not scared

Are you there? Are you coming with me?

Be **careful**! Be careful of the cars!

Quick – cross the road now!

Where's Poppy? There she is. She's with Jessica.

But who are all the **other** people? There are so **many** people here. And so many cars and bikes.

Are you **scared**? Don't be scared.

I'm not scared. I'm **never** scared.

WHAT'S THAT?! IS IT A VERY BIG DOG?!

RUN!!

From: The Learn English Activity Book for Children

MARK'S HOLIDAYS – True or False?

My name's Mark. There are five of us in my family – my parents, my older sister, my little brother and me. We live in a big, noisy **modern** city. My parents work very hard at work and my sister and I work very hard at school. So we love going on holiday!

My family goes on holiday once or twice a year. We usually go in the summer, in August, because that's when the long school holidays are. And sometimes we go away at Christmas too, to stay with my grandparents in their big house in a different, nicer city.

I like going on holiday in the summer because it's hot. We often go to the seaside and it's warm enough to swim in the sea. But my mum doesn't really like going to the beach. She says it's too hot and too boring. She likes staying in old hotels in beautiful towns and cities. She loves good food and she wants to eat at a different restaurant every evening. My little brother is only three. He's not interested in restaurants. He usually wants to go to the park to play on the swings. My sister is sixteen now. She says she wants to go on holiday with her friends next year. My dad always has fun on holiday. He's happy not to be at work!

1. Mark is the youngest child in his family.   **T / F**
2. His parents both like their jobs.   **T / F**
3. They go on holiday every year.   **T / F**
4. They all like doing the **same** things on holiday.   **T / F**
5. Mark's grandparents don't live in the **countryside**.   **T / F**
6. Mark's sister is lazy.   **T / F**
7. Mark loves his city.   **T / F**
8. Mark's mum doesn't want to go to the beach every summer.   **T / F**
9. Everyone likes hot weather!   **T / F**
10. Mark stays with his grandparents in their flat once a year.   **T / F**

From: Read English with Ben - 1

14. Present

The day after the last day of school was the first day of the summer holidays. But Ben didn't feel excited. He felt unhappy.

He **lay** on his bed in his bedroom with a book. But he didn't read the book. He thought about all those years at primary school. He thought about his friends.

His mum **called** him. "It's lunchtime, Ben! Come downstairs!"

Ben **sighed**. He went downstairs to the dining room. He **started** to say: "I'm not hungry, mum. I don't want any lunch." But then he stopped. What was that on the table? It was a **parcel**. Was it a **present**? For him?

46

www.ingramcontent.com/pod-product-compliance
Lightning Source LLC
LaVergne TN
LVHW020436080526
838202LV00055B/5210